THINK OUTSIDE THE BOX CONCERNING MARRIAGE

RICHARD SZALECKI

Pronounced, "Sah-LEH-key"

WestBow
PRESS®
A DIVISION OF THOMAS NELSON
& ZONDERVAN

WestBow Press books may be ordered through booksellers or by contacting:

WestBow Press
A Division of Thomas Nelson & Zondervan
1663 Liberty Drive
Bloomington, IN 47403
www.westbowpress.com
844-714-3454

All scripture references are taken from the Simplified King James Version of the Bible, copyright 2022 by Barbour Publishing, Inc. Used with permission.

ISBN: 978-1-9736-9986-6 (sc)
ISBN: 978-1-9736-9987-3 (e)

Library of Congress Control Number: 2023910268

Print information available on the last page.

WestBow Press rev. date: 06/28/2023

CONTENTS

ACKNOWLEDGMENTS

This book is dedicated to my wife Cheryl along with my pastor, Scott Veroneau of Community Life Church in Gulf Breeze, Florida. I love them so much. They have been so supportive of me. I am also thankful for the presence of Community Life Church which is my home church. It is the best church I have ever been part of. You're encouraging and a big blessing!

"Rick has a great love for and working knowledge of the Word of God. The way he holds scripture allows him to discover points of connection between scripture that may have never been considered. As a result, deeper themes are uncovered and the sacred text continues to reveal."

Scott Veroneau / Lead Pastor
Community Life Church

PREFACE

I was interested in writing this book on marriage in mid-December 2022. I was home alone. I texted an outline for my book to my pastor, Scott Veroneau of Community Life Church in Gulf Breeze, Florida. He texted me back and said, "This book is ready to go as-is!" That was quite the encouragement! I told him I had to add some things to the book to fill it out. This is the final product.

It's exciting when someone looks over an outline and says it is a book as-is. It's a big boost of confidence to me. My heart is to share the spiritual aspects of marriage. It think it's really important to share the proper role of Adam and Eve and also incorporate the truth that the husband and wife are to serve each other in the marriage relationship. I explain how marriage is a picture of Christ and the church. I also talk about how important communication is in marriage.

Couples of every age group can grow in their commitments and relationships by applying the principles of this book.

INTRODUCTION

Marriage is a mystery! I have said amusingly that it's time to divorce when you figure out the mystery.

Marriage is a RELATIONSHIP OF COMMITMENT and a LOVE RELATIONSHIP including cohabitation between a man and a woman. The ceremony itself, the engagement and courtship periods leading up to it are exciting. Then there is the honeymoon after the wedding ceremony. It's all exciting. I remember my father remarrying at 72 years old. Mom passed away at age 66 in 1999. Dad was a widower for 2-1/2 years. I received a call from Dad one Saturday morning. He asked me If I wanted to be his Best Man. I was thrilled that he asked me. I accepted his invitation. Dad and I stood at the church altar that Fall. He turned to me before the ceremony and said, "I don't care how many times I do this. It still makes me nervous!" I understand that.

A radio commercial from years ago said a Hollywood Wedding was like a Car Wash- five minutes and the whole thing was over! We hear stories of marriages that don't last all too often. Let's compare marriages to car washes. Most of the Automatic Car Washes I've been to give a choice of three washes: The Express, The Intermediate or the Deluxe Wash. The Express Wash cleans the outside of the car, rinse it and dry it. An Intermediate Wash will clean the car and the tires and make the tires shine. The Deluxe Wash will clean everything outside and underneath the car, plus provide a sealant to protect the paint.

Marriage is like that Deluxe Car Wash. The commitment and the investment is the deepest. Marriage takes more time than living together or being engaged. Marriage will turn you inside out. Marriage will also refine you, make you more loving, purer and more of what God intended you to be.

God didn't intend for us to be alone. Men, God gave us helpers fit for us. That's a key-FIT FOR US. The scripture says we can marry who we want but only in the Lord. When considering marriage we can ask this question, "Is my husband or wife fit for me?" Also ask, "Did God put us together?"

Matthew 19:6b says, "Therefore what God has joined together let no man separate." Getting married is a bit different than going through the car wash. God chooses our mates. I know this by my inner witness, my spirit. God shows us the right mate and confirms it over and over. It's also confirmed by the fruit that is produced.

Compatibility is not the biggest issue. Chuck and Barb Snyder wrote a book called, "Incompatibility: Grounds For a Great Marriage." I learned some character from being incompatible. I eventually turned off the television set on Sunday afternoons to spend time with my family. I gave up something I loved for the greater good of my family. I occupied my children so my wife could nap.

Let's go further into this Car Wash analogy. The scripture says, "And they two shall be one flesh."- Matthew 19:5b. The term "flesh" means 'body." The two shall become one body. There is significance here. Just sharing bodies is like going through the Express Car Wash. The body is being cleaned and nourished but two dimensions of oneness are still missing. Many couples divorce because they're sharing only their bodies.

Sharing bodies and souls is like going through the Intermediate Car Wash. Couples share their bodies and some soul issues and still miss a dimension in marriage.

Our marriages need the Deluxe Car Wash-spirit, soul and body. God desires our marriages to be pure, whole and cleansed. This happens when our spirit is controlled by the Holy Spirit and our spirit then controls our souls and bodies. The spiritual dimension is missing in so many marriages today.

This is not the book for you if you were looking for a sex primer. "Think Outside the Box Concerning Marriage" focuses on some issues of marriage that other books don't focus on:

- Adam and Eve were corrected by God in the Garden so that neither of them would have an independent spirit. This is critically important for our marriages.-Genesis 3
- The husband and wife are to serve one another.- Ephesians 5:21. Even though the husband is the head of the wife the headship is more for responsibility and accountability to God. The husband does not wear the pants in the family. Mutual submission between husband and his woman makes the marriage work.
- Marriage is a picture of Christ and the church. He lives in us as believers, and He lives through our marriages. We are of His flesh and of His bones. Christ lives through us and gives resurrection life to our marriages.
- Good, through communication is important in our marriages. It assists our spirits so that we mature, and our prayers are answered.
- Who can we marry considering the spiritual climate in our world?

This book focuses completely on spiritual values that make a marriage honorable and successful. I'm all for stronger, long-lasting marriages. Looking at some deeper, issues will increase your chances for meaning, happiness, oneness that you are looking for with your marriage partner and a deepening of your faith in Christ. God bless you.

- Richard Szalecki

A PICTURE OF MARRIAGE

Let me get this objection out of the way right now: I'm on my second marriage. Some of you may tune me out right away. Let me answer. I was married for almost 29 years. I learned some things. The biggest lesson I learned was that marriage was a good thing! It's just that my marriage failed. It's not important to know all the reasons and who is to blame. John Maxwell said that husbands and wives share problems and go through things that no one else goes through. I sat under the ministry of David Robinson, pastor of Community Christian Church in Nottingham, Maryland in the Baltimore suburbs from 2010-2013. He conducted a series on marriage and said that marriage presented some of the greatest challenges and had some of the highest payoffs or rewards for couples. I think Lynn Hiles said it best and with the best humor. He said, "Love is blind, but marriage is an eye opener." This is so true! Marriage will turn you inside out. If there was ever a relationship that will cost you your independent identity, marriage is it.

I want to go back and talk about the days when I was independent, the days before I was married. I was 19 in the Summer of 1974. I had just finished my education at Community College. I was working at a discount department store that summer and getting ready to transition to four year college. The legal drinking age was lowered in Maryland from 21 to 18 on July 1, 1974. It was PARTY TIME! I was rarely home. I made my bed just three times all summer. I went clubbing with my friends to Sea Gull Inn or Hollywood Palace at least every Wednesday and Saturday. I raced my 1967 Chevy Nova Station Wagon up to 90 miles per hour on country back roads. I got off of work at 9 pm most nights I worked, went out and didn't return home until 2:30 am. Dirty clothes went into a pile for Mom to wash. I had responsibilities to help cut the grass in my family's big yard. I didn't always do it. I dated some. I did what I wanted and when I wanted to do it. I had nearly no cares in the world.

My marriage in 1979 changed all that. "Take your shoes off at the door," my new wife yelled. "Take out the trash…This is how you iron." I already knew how to iron because Mom taught me how to iron. I bowled duckpins on Saturday mornings when I was growing up. My mother told me if I wanted to look presentable with clean, ironed clothes when I bowled I had to learn to iron my bowling shirt. I always felt proud wearing my pressed shirt.

Marriage changes us so that we learn new habits, unlearn old ones and do things differently. We face the same things in our marriages we do at work and at church: "We've always done it this way. I'm not changing." It's not easy to break old habits and establish new ones. Arguments and fights can break out during adjustment periods. Lynn Hiles also suggested that each new married couple should live in a trailer the first few years of marriage. That way they can fight and throw things at each other and not worry about losing the house's value.

I'll never forget the woman who spoke in my church some years ago and said, "I was newly married and I woke up and said, 'Who is this strange man sleeping next to me in my bed?'" I went through that about six weeks into my former marriage. The adjustment was funny, yet uncomfortable and even overwhelming all at the same time. A lot of new relationships are like that.

Marriage takes commitment and the commitment sustains the marriage. Feelings come and go. I can remember days of not having feelings for my former wife. PLEASE DO NOT READ INTO ANYTHING TOO DEEPLY. THIS IS AN ILLUSTRATION, NOT AN INDICTMENT OF EITHER PARTY. Couples who have been married for any length of time can experience this. I would pray and tell God how I felt. God would say, "Rub her back," or, "Put the clothes in the washing machine for her," or, "Go in and check on the children." When I did what God told me to do my feelings would change into renewed joy and love. It was always a wonderful feeling to listen to God when my feelings weren't where they should have been. God will change our attitudes of anger toward our spouse, too, when we open ourselves up to Him in prayer.

I think we put too much emphasis on being married. I was married at 24. Part of the reason I got married was that I would be an old, unmarried man at 27. Face it-people get married for all different kinds of reasons. Benjamin Disraeli was Prime Minister of Britain in the 1800's. His wife used to say, "I married him for his money!" He used to say, "I married her for her looks!" It was said they had a wonderful marriage. They loved each other and they didn't take themselves too seriously. Many of us have a problem, though. We put too much emphasis on marriages and we fail to live up to its perceived ideals. We fight, we argue and we jockey for position in leadership and we fail. What can we do about it? How can we make our marriages more successful?

BACK TO ADAM AND EVE

Here is Adam in the Garden of Eden. God has Adam name all of the animals and God then says, "It is not good for man should be alone; I will make him a help suitable for him."- Genesis 2:18. The Lord caused Adam to fall into a deep sleep. The Lord took a rib from Adam's side and formed Eve. He brought the woman unto the man and Adam took a "ribbing" from Eve ever since!

Adam and Eve were naked and unashamed. It wasn't because they didn't have clothes and he was the man and she was the woman. It's because they were relating spirit-to-spirit! They were in fellowship with God and each other. It was beautiful, or, as my daughter called it when she was five, "boo-fitul". My daughter was and is precious. We were created by God as spiritual beings. Watchman Nee in his classic book, "The Spiritual Man", says that man is a three-part being. We are a spirit being that possesses a soul and lives in a body. The spirit has three parts: worship, which connects us to God; conscience, which functions to tell us right from wrong, and intuition, which allows us to determine the manner of spirit in another person. Our souls encompass the mind, will and emotions. Our body contains all of this. I will go as far as to say, "We are God's house."

I want to point out some things here. God made a helper FIT for Adam (emphasis mine). Many of us have not quite understood what that meant. Many men pick a woman for themselves based on what they THINK is fit for them. "Oh, she makes me feel good about myself all the time," "She's so good looking," or, "I love her for her money," and so on. By this reasoning we fall short of God's desire for us and we have only a partially glorious marriage relationship, if that. Moreover, people grow and change over time. A partner gets sick at 35 and goes on Social Security Disability. A husband loses his well-paying job at 47 and has to tap into his savings. An economic downturn happens on their home loan, they lose their home and they file for bankruptcy.

Turmoil occurs naturally and it is exacerbated when the husband and his woman are not joined together by God. I learned in my former marriage that negative circumstances reveal the deeper issues that are inside of us. Some of our circumstances are caused by us not taking care of our bodies and for not being responsible at work. When we are married and we have a partner completely of our own choosing we don't just grapple with the issues at hand and on the surface. God digs deep down also into the character issues that got us there in the first place. Revealing those character issues takes time sometimes. Our problems we cause can be deep rooted and long lasting.

Zig Ziglar was a popular sales trainer, life motivator and author. I love the way he described Adam and Eve. "God confronted Adam about eating the forbidden fruit off the tree of knowledge of good and evil and Adam said, 'The woman made me do it.' The Lord confronted the woman and she said, 'The serpent made me do it.' Now, the serpent didn't have a leg to stand on!"

We pawn off out responsibilities and accountability to our partner and even the devil. We don't stand up and take responsibility for our actions. We do a little "CYA" like Adam and Eve did. "CYA" stands for "Cover Your Anatomy". I said it all right, didn't I? Adam and Eve sewed fig leaves together themselves because a Singer sewing machine was sold out at Walmart back then. Those fig leaves they sewed together were made to cover their backsides, too. Think about fig leaves. They're lush, big and green. They get brittle, turn brown and crack. Leaves drop to the ground. Adam and Eve could have run into a hanging tree branch while walking in the Garden and the fig leaf apron could have torn. They would have exposed their aprons again. Many of us apply our own solutions to our problems only to revisit the same problems again without solving them.

God sought out Adam before and after Adam and Eve took the forbidden fruit because God wanted fellowship. Fellowship is communion. Communion is common union with God. Here is my interpretation of fellowship from 1 John 1:7, "But if we walk in the light as He is in the light, we have fellowship (communion, common union) with one another, and the blood of Jesus Christ cleanses us from all (every) sin. (Everything in parentheses is my emphasis.)" Sin doesn't just mean our offenses against God. I researched deeply and found out that sin also means to miss the mark so as to not share in the prize. The prize is to walk in the Spirit and let the Spirit of God be our guide; and let our spirit control our soul and body. To let our soul and not our spirit direct our lives is to miss the mark and not share in the prize, which is knowing God in fellowship, communion and intimacy.

God supplies our need when we walk in the Spirit and have our spirits control our minds and bodies. I alluded to Zig Ziglar's comical explanation of Adam and Eve's transgression, which is to say they bent beyond what God told them to do.

Here is why God disciplined Adam and Eve for what they did: God told the serpent, "On your belly you shall go and you shall eat dust all the days of your life."- Genesis 3:14. God took the right of the serpent away from speaking his life into the woman and also into the man by extension. He told the woman that the man would rule over her. God told Adam that Adam would eat of the fruit of the ground by his own efforts and not by the Spirit of God. God cursed the ground for Adam's sake, and here's why: The serpent was made to crawl in the dust and the dust was cursed. This was so that anytime the man or the woman engaged the serpent in the dust realm Adam and Eve would see and experience the curse.

The serpent has NO POWER OVER US unless we operate in our soulish realm. Maybe you remember Jesus saying to Peter,

"Get behind me Satan! You are a stumbling block to Me, for you appreciate the things that are of men, but not the things that are of God."-Matthew 16:33. It's important to realize Jesus isn't calling Peter a devil. Jesus is saying that Peter was engaging Jesus from the realm of his soul and that kind of engagement was allowing the devil to try to take a foothold in the situation. This is the danger of living in the soulish realm and letting it rule. The devil can operate in the mind of men's souls only if we let him.

Here's why God disciplined Adam and Eve like He did. It was to eliminate an independent spirit in each one of them. God said to Eve, "Your desire shall be toward your husband."-Genesis 3:16. Eve engaged the serpent in his temptation. "And when the woman saw that the tree (of knowledge of good and evil) was good for food and that it was pleasant to the eyes and a tree to be desired to make one wise, she took it some of its fruit and ate and gave also to her husband, and he ate."-Genesis 3:6. Eve engaged the serpent at a soulish level, using just her mind, will and emotions. That is what is meant by soulish. This led to her independence from God. Her response was to be embarrassed. Adam operated in the soul realm, too, when she gave some of the fruit to Adam and he ate it.

Again, God said to Eve, "Your desire shall be for your husband and he shall rule over you."-Gen. 3:16. Many people take the word, "rule" the wrong way, taking it to mean power. Many men think they are the boss at home. Rule speaks to me more about accountability to God than it does about who's the boss. Let's be very clear: POWER IS NOT LOVE. God called husbands and wives to love one another. God called all of us to love one another. I believe accountability to God gives us power to love and serve. Accountability is a better fitting spiritual word here. Moreover, the scripture says that we all will have to give account of ourselves to Christ. I'll talk more about this when I discuss Ephesians 5.

Overall, God is giving correction to eliminate the independent spirit in Adam and Eve. God no longer wanted Eve to operate in the soulish realm. She did it once. That was enough. God wanted

Adam to not reap of the fruit of the ground of his own strength. God wanted Adam to love and serve Eve. He wanted Eve's attention and focus to be on Adam. The Lord wanted both of their attention to be on Him. This is proper operation of a marriage: to operate with your spirit controlling your souls and your bodies, and being submissive to God for love, direction and fellowship. This is what works at home. God spoke to the man and the woman in correction to prevent an independent spirit in each of them.

I have to extend this beyond marriage to interpersonal male/female relationships. This is just as important as anything else I said. "Nevertheless, neither is the man independent of the woman not woman independent of the man, in the Lord."-1 Corinthians 11:11, New International Version. We Christians need to learn this truth and apply it correctly. As we learn that Christian men and women are interdependent with each other as it was spiritually in the Garden of Eden, more men and women will be prepared for healthy marriages.

MARRIAGE'S PROPER ALIGNMENT AS TOLD IN EPHESIANS 5

The popular thought about the marriage passage in Ephesians 5 is that the husband is the head of the woman and the woman has to submit to her husband. People in the church generally believe that the husband's role is power and authority. Have a very interesting illustration that was given to my church by Pastor Albert Meyers in the 1980's. He said that authority was like using a bar of soap. The faster you use it the faster it is used up." In other words, we can boss people only so much until the other people stop allowing it. If the husband makes all the decisions and does not allow input from his wife the wife clams up and the marriage goes stale. Many marriages fail because the husband uses this kind of authority by bossing and controlling his woman all the time. Apostle Paul talks about the contrast of two kinds of authority. He says, "Not that we have dominion over your faith, but we are helpers of your joy, for by faith you stand."-2 Corinthians 1:24. Lording his testimony over others' faith is something Paul sees as "control". Control drives people away. When we are examples to our wives our women love us much more easily. Then we operate in the Spirit with our spirit controlling us. Thant's wisdom.

I thought I had to wear the pants in the family the first 20 years I was married the first time around. I was taught this constantly in church. I thought I had to grow into that role. It made me feel somewhat macho. My woman and I were at odds on a lot of issues.

I limited her feedback on some decisions and I made some wrong decisions based on my attitudes. I had thought she had to submit to my rule no matter what. That all changed beginning one Sunday morning in 2000. I turned a Christian program on the radio while I was on my way to my Church Service. The host talked about Ephesians 5. He said, "Ephesians 5 says that the husband is the head of this wife but it also says before the marriage passage begins that the husband and wife are to submit themselves to one another in the fear of Christ." (-Ephesians 5:21)

This truth opened my eyes! I woke up to the fact that I was misusing my role as a husband. I confessed my mistake to God. I began to submit to my wife. Doing this felt uneasy at times. I made myself vulnerable. I thought my married male friends would reject me. My first steps were unsteady. I don't think my first wife and I ever got on the same page concerning authority and accountability. I'm not placing blame on her. We were both inculcated with wrong attitudes given by church teaching and tradition. These teachings hindered our ability to change and accept this new truth. It's nobody's business why we divorced. I discovered as I dealt with my divorce was that marriage was a good thing. I moved forward with my life with a clear conscience.

THE CORRECT THOUGHTS ON MARRIAGE FROM EPHESIANS 5

I'm going to discuss this entire passage on marriage verse-by-verse:
"*21…submitting yourselves to one another in the fear of God. 22… Wives, submit yourselves unto your own husbands, as to the Lord. 23… For the husband is the head of the wife, even as Christ is the head of the church, and He is the Savior of the body. 24…Therefore as the church is subject to Christ, so let the wives be to their own husbands in everything. 25…Husbands, love your wives, even as Christ loved the church, and gave himself for it, 26…that he might sanctify it and cleanse it by the washing of water by the word, 27…that he might present it to himself a glorious church, not having spot or wrinkle, or any such thing, but that it should be holy and without blemish. 28…So men ought to love their wives as their own bodies. He who loves his wife loves himself. 29…For no man ever hated his own flesh, but nourishes and cherishes it, even as the Lord the church. 30…For we are members of his body, of His flesh and of His bones. 31…For this reason a man shall leave his father and mother, and be joined unto his wife, and the two of them shall be one flesh. 32…This is a great mystery, but I speak concerning Christ and the church. 33…Nevertheless, let every one of you in particular so love his wife even as himself and the wife see that she reverence her husband.*"-Ephesians 5:21-33.

I already covered verse 21, "Submitting yourselves to one another in the fear of God." Paul addressed the church at large when he shared that verse. Then he turned to address the most important relationship on earth, the relationship between husband and wife. Husbands and their women spend more time together than any other relationship on earth. God blessed the relationship and He called it holy, which means "set apart". The Lord values this relationship most highly. Paul's saying of submitting ourselves to one another in a marital relationship is Paul's and God's own heart in restoring the marriage relationship and all of the body of Christ as it was in the time of Adam and Eve before the Fall.

"*22...Wives, submit yourselves to your own husbands, as unto the Lord.*"

Paul addressed the women first just like God addressed Eve first in the Garden of Eden. Eve was the one who was led astray to engage the serpent in the soulish realm. Eve then got Adam to eat of the forbidden fruit. This illustrates how influential wives can be. Wives are shown to be the weaker of the two vessels as Paul describes later in my text because the woman engaged with then gave in to the serpent's guile. Paul sounded like God's voice in that he wanted to eliminate the wife's independent spirit.

"*23...For the husband is the head of the wife, even as Christ is the head of the church: and He is the Savior of the body.*"

I submit that the husband is the head of the wife for the sake of accountability to God and not of authority. Paul talked about both partners serving each other. When they do, they operate by the Spirit working through their spirits and their spirits putting their souls and bodies under subjection. An independent spirit has no place to operate in either one of them. The husband and his woman operate in love. Paul opens up this passage to illustrate Christ and the church. The marital relationship is a smaller part of the bigger picture. This whole allegory is about Christ and the church! The life of Christ needs to be lived out in life's most important institution, the home.

Notice that Paul said that Jesus was the Savior of the body. Remembering the Garden account, Adam and Eve sewed fig leaves together when their eyes were opened and they saw that they were naked. What they really did was cover up themselves before God.

The Lord did something to cover them more permanently. He made clothing from animal skins for the two of them. The outfits were more permanent but they were not everlasting. This speaks indirectly about the Law, too. With His birth, death and resurrection Christ really is the Savior of the body. This means something far deeper, though. Adam's and Eve's bodies were affected by their bad decisions made in their soulish realms. Here's another note: Jesus is the second Adam! When our spirits are in communion and fellowship with our spirits our bodies are preserved. They're not only preserved in health; they're preserved from acts of our souls that get us in trouble.

24…"*Therefore as the church is subject unto Christ, so let the wives be to their husbands in everything.*"

This verse upsets a lot of people. Wives say, "This means that I have to submit to my husband in everything? That's a big risk. It's a problem if our husbands are ogres or they think they have to be the boss all the time. This inhibits communication. I as a wife cannot give all my necessary input into the important decisions I have to make. I sense some of the decisions he makes are wrong. I can also tell with my intuition that some of his decisions are wrong. I feel stymied sometimes and he gets us in trouble."

I understand. It's a big risk to submit yourselves to your husbands in this way. Remember something, men and women: Remember what a husband is. He tends to his wife. He is responsible for two people plus any children that come along. I need to dive into what a husband is. To say that a husband is a partner to his wife is just scratching the surface.

I found a beautiful website worth checking out: vinesofthey aravalley.au. The website gives a beautiful, more comprehensive illustration of what a husband is. Here is a list of attributes:

- Emotionally mature
- Acknowledges your flaws
- Manages conflicts well
- Trustworthy

- Prioritises your relationship
- Appreciates your excellent and negative qualities
- Considers you in major and little decision making
- Growth oriented
- Common beliefs and values
- Always communicates with you
- Plans to marry you

These attributes are absolutely wonderful! They speak of something to me. They are all spiritual values. The website's author is saying what I am saying and using different words. Look at some of these attributes: trustworthiness, communication, affection, properly using your emotions, sharing important core values and serving her. If the husband's spirit is submitted to God he walks in the Spirit and alignment happens a whole lot better between the husband and wife. This is wonderful! Walking together keeps the partners from walking soulishly and from fulfilling their selfish desires.

It's a great big deal for the woman to submit to her husband in everything. Love and trust for him are so important. The man has to be like a husbandman who tends to his vine full of grapes and bring forth the best crops. He must get his life in order first and he has to serve his woman. When he walks in his spirit having control under the leadership of God's Spirit, he can see more spiritual values and even see things that need adjusting in the relationship. He can then do it with a spirit of meekness and self-control. Mistakes will be made, mind you. Like vine dressing, pruning out that he might present it to himself things that will bring forth better crops.

25…"Husbands, love your wives, even as Christ loved the church, and gave himself for it, 26…that he might sanctify and cleanse it with the washing of water by the word, 27…that He might present it to himself a glorious church, not having spot, or wrinkle, or any such thing, but that it should be holy and without blemish."

How did Christ show His love for the church? The scripture says He came not to be served but to serve. He also gave His life as a ransom to many. A good husband will find it costs him everything for him to have a good marriage. This is God's discipline. Notice I am not saying it is God's correction. Part of God's discipline is in pointing out things we do wrong, like miscommunication. No one communicates perfectly all the time. Hebrews 13:16, KJV says, "But to do good and to communicate forget not, for with such sacrifices God is well pleased." God may discipline us if communication with our spouses is lacking, but let me be clear in saying that God is not standing right next to us with a whip and ready for us to mess up. He is with us like a loving Father. Discipline is administered only as necessary and only with the amount needed commensurate with the offense.

(Visiting again…) *"Not having spot, or wrinkle, or any such thing;"*

I dated this girl. We had a really good relationship. I said to her on her first date, "You have a clean slate with me. Your past is forgiven." This did wonders for her! She had a clear conscience. I felt built up. I felt good about the relationship because of her response to my actions. Our relationship grew.

As we all know, issues come up in any relationship. As we dated, we had to learn boundaries. We needed to learn how to handle stress in each other as a couple. We also needed to learn how to handle each other's personal quirks.

Having no spot or wrinkle is very important to us. Christ has not only forgiven all of our sins, He remembers them no more. Ref.: Hebrews 10:17. Why do so many people have a sin mentality when the Father through Jesus wiped out our sins! We who are believers in Jesus' sanctifying grace have had our sins blotted out. Why do we keep bringing up the things of our sins over and over? Jesus was the covering of our sins before the Father. Husbands are supposed to cover their wives to present them as a glorious church without spot or wrinkle. This comes by the husband's service toward his woman. It also comes by applying the love and forgiveness of God through Christ.

I am not talking about being "religious" here. I am talking about being real and authentic. We can only do this with our spirits and having them be under control of the Spirit of God.

28... "*So ought men to love their wives as their own bodies. He who loves his wife loves himself.*" *29...* "*For no man ever yet hated his own flesh; but nourishes it and cherishes it, even as the Lord the church:*"

I am breaking down this verse into pieces now. We're getting to the meat of this, the real meaning of marriage. Marriage is about Christ and the church. God created Adam and Eve. The foundational unit where God desires to bless His people is the family. This is wonderful. The family is also the foundational unit of the church.

The man nourishes and cherishes his flesh like the Lord loves and cherishes the church. Our Lord cherishes His church through service. He laid down His life for us. He served us while here on earth. Jesus also did everything by His Spirit under the direction of God's Spirit. This is what the husband does. He serves his woman, and he serves her because he loves her. Those who serve their wives out of obligation or duty miss the mark.

30... "*for we are members of his body, of his flesh and of his bones.*"

1) "We are members of His body..."

This verse is electrifying. We are called into one body. "There is one body and one Spirit, even as you are called,..."-Ephesians 4:4.

THE BODY IS CHRIST

"Now you (collectively) are Christ's body, and individually (you are) members of it (each with his own special own special purpose and function)."-1 Corinthians 12:27. This is not to say that God won't bless someone if they are single. Not everyone is called to be married. Matthew 19 also spells this out. Single people are able to hear from God just like married people. Married people have the ability to have and raise children if they want to.

2) *"...of his flesh..."*

This is REMARKABLE! Understanding what this means is life changing. The scriptures clearly point this out.

"Therefore, from now on we recognize no man according to the flesh. Yes, though we have known Christ according to the flesh, yet we know longer know now hereafter ven though we have known Christ by the flesh, yet now we know Him in this way no longer."-2 Corinthians 5:16. Paul says that the apostles know NO ONE by the flesh. The flesh represents the first Adam, who fell. Paul now recognizes believers just as I described earlier in this book, spirit beings who possess a soul and live in a body. We who are believers know Jesus in a different way, a life-giving Spirit.-1 Corinthians 15:45. By this, Jesus is the Second Adam. Jesus never gave in to sin like Adam did.

Romans 6:8-9, "Now if we have died in Christ, we believe that we shall also live with Him, knowing that Christ, having been raised from the dead dies no more; death has no more dominion over him." This is tremendous communion, and when I am talking about communion I am not talking about the bread and the wine. I am talking about our communion with God. Christ was dead to sin but alive to God. We render our bodies dead to sin through water baptism. Water baptism has a positive side. "The similar symbol to this baptism, which also now saves us (not the putting away of the filth of the flesh, but the answer of a good conscience toward God) through the resurrection of Jesus Christ..."-1 Peter 3:21. Baptism has no negativity in it at all.

I am going into such detail about marriage and the resurrected Christ to show we serve a risen Lord and Savior. By Jesus being the Second Adam we can call on and serve a resurrected Savior who is without sin and who will preserve our bodies.

3) *"…and of his bones."*

If you really want to be blessed, consider this: Like as Adam was put into a deep sleep and God took a rib and formed Eve, a Roman soldier took a spear and thrust it into Jesus' side after He was dead. God, through Jesus deep sleep, His death, formed the church! That's exciting to me. The prophet Elisha died. Someone touched Elisha's bones and that person came back to life. Jesus Himself was flesh and bones. When we realize that Jesus wasn't just a spirit when He came back to life but had come in a resurrected body, these same bones gave us life. Jesus told Thomas to thrust his hands into Jesus' side. Thomas did and what an exclamation Thomas shared! To touch Jesus' bones in the likeness of His resurrection realm is life that is imparted to us. Take courage! The point is the resurrected Christ is in the middle of our marriage relationships.

31… "For this cause shall a man leave his father and mother, and shall be joined unto his wife, and the two of them shall be one flesh. 32… This is a great mystery, but I speak concerning Christ and the church."

For what cause? For Christ and the Church. "Joined" is an important word. Just as Adam and Eve were joined to each other our marriages are joined to the resurrected Christ. That is the true picture of Christian marriage and it is life giving. Another word for "joining" is "cleaving". Too many married people don't make a clean break from their upbringing to join with their newly married partners. "Cleaving" means to cut off and make a clean break from the past and adhere to the new relationship, the marriage. "Marriage is honorable in all and the bed undefiled."-5:16. Some men are "Mama's Boys". Some women never make that clean break from their parents and cleave to their husbands. These behaviors negatively affect their marriages. These marriages can be affected so much that the couple winds up in Divorce Court.

I joke sometimes that marriage is a mystery and it's time to divorce when you figure it out. Figuring out the mystery is nothing more than pride. The marriage relationship is so dynamic that it costs us everything we have. It affects all our lives as married couples. God called us to love and serve one another. So many things happen in our lives: we marry, one partner loses a job, one partner's mother dies, a baby is born, the husband goes on Disability, and so on. Life has so much mystery to it. We need to be connected to the Resurrected Christ in every circumstance.

Ephesians 5:33 says, *"Nevertheless let every one of you in particular so love his wife even as himself and the wife see that she reverence her husband." Jesus said to the Pharisees in Matthew 22:39, "You shall love your neighbor as yourself."* Jesus said that the Law and the Prophets hang on this and on loving the Lord God with all your heart, soul, mind and strength. Our wives should be treated no differently. The wife is to be loved along with and next to God.

The wife is to reverence her husband. Strong's Concordance says that to reverence is to "be in awe of". Granted, respect must be earned. We cannot as husbands and men force our wives to be in awe of us. Women and men can be attracted by each other's looks in the beginning of a relationship. Women grow in love for their husbands by the husband's character. "He loves me," "He respects me," and, "He puts me first all the time," are just three of the things women in love say about their spouses. Men, you are the husbands. You tend to your women, your wives. Show the way by serving them. People always respond in kind to how you treat them.

WORKING IT ALL OUT IN MARRIAGE WITH PRACTICALITY

We need to work out our marriage relationships with some practicality.

"Then his (Job's) wife said to him, do you still retain your integrity? Curse God and die!"- Job 2:9.

I'm bringing up Job here and a real-life situation in marriage. Have you ever taken close study of women, especially wives? They're survivors! Job's wife witnessed and experienced everything that Job went through. I'm sure she was devastated. There are things that happen in our lives that are beyond our ability to control. We get furious, upset, depressed, despondent and demoralized.

Women are survivors. When the husband loses his job or has a stroke, the wife goes back to work. If the family runs too short on money, she finds ways to raise funds and catch up on the bills. Wives are the primary caregivers of the children when the children are sick. Wives feel the responsibility of holding things together when things go awry.

This happens in the church. Why do we have so many more women than men in the churches? Pastors were preaching about Hell so much two and more generations ago. The messages were effective. But pastors preached about Hell so much that it scared the men out of the churches. The wives kept coming to church in part since then to hold things together at home and get directions for their lives and households. Women were scared, too, and this was their security, to attend church and hopefully receive some encouragement.

Women play an important part in men's lives; more important than men think!

Job's wife said the expedient thing to her husband, "Curse God and die." We chide Job's wife for saying that. That's just not the case. There are times when our integrity does not solve our problems by itself. We want to prove that we behaved ourselves even in our afflictions. We do this many times to try to gain approval of God and our mates while using our own strength. Job's integrity was found in that he never cursed God. Sure, his friends tried to comfort him. Job realized what he should do at some point. He lifted his complaint to God. Integrity involves more than outward behavior; it involves inner attitudes. We many or may not see the inner working of those inner attitudes. But God sees.

Job's problem in life, if you will, was that he was complacent. He had more possessions than anybody. He had 10 happy children. I can tell you I had wealth, and it was all taken away like what happened to Job. Many people suffer through this. The problem is that we get too complacent when we accumulate certain wealth and we become too well off financially. Our wealth becomes our castle and our tower of protection. We feel so strong in our wealth that our thought life becomes a place where we feel no one can touch it-or us.

Things would have been different with Job and his wife if Job took the time to prepare his wife for bad times. 1 Peter 3:7 says, "Likewise, husbands, dwell with them (your wives) according to knowledge, giving honor unto the wife as unto the weaker vessel, and as being heirs together of the grace of life, that your prayers are not hindered."

Life I said, we men don't take time with our wives to prepare them for emergencies. We are to dwell with our wives according to knowledge. Husbands can kiss and hug their wives while going out the door to work in the morning and the husband can say, "Don't forget to pray for me at work today, Honey!"

She says smilingly, "I won't forget, Honey," and she kisses him. The wife then prays, "God, please give my hubby a good day at work. Amen."

Her prayers didn't get answered. Why? Her husband didn't go into enough detail about what was going on at work. He and his boss were having a tiff. They weren't seeing each other eye-to-eye. His boss sent him home early. He lost some pay. His ego and hers were bruised.

We need to pray for emergencies, and we need to pray with intelligence. Suppose the husband said to his wife, "Pray for me today, Honey. My boss and I aren't seeing things eye-to-eye at work. I need you to pray today." The wife would have prayed knowing what was going on at her husband's job. More fervor would have gone into her prayers. The chances that God would have addressed the situation as work would have increased. God doesn't answer our prayers sometimes so He can correct something about us. PRAY WITH INTELLIGENCE.

Husbands, let your women know what is going on with your lives. This brings intimacy and increases faith. Your wives will respond accordingly with intelligence. More prayers will be answered. The two of you will become closer. It's a WIN-WIN for you both.

"Likewise, husbands, dwell with them according to knowledge, giving honor unto to wife as to the weaker vessel, and as being heirs together of the grace of life."-The 1 Peter 3:7. Let's look at the wife being the weaker vessel. Our natural eye sees that our wives are not as physically strong as we are. They also get easily distracted sometimes. Us men do, too. We're not immune. These distractions can be from communication problems. Men think they have to wear the pants in the family. They don't communicate effectively as a result. While looking out for the family our women are there to be our helpmeet. To deny them the opportunity and responsibility to be a helpmeet is to open the door for the wife to seek outside help to solve problems without the husband's knowledge. This problem goes all the way back to the Garden of Eden when Eve was deceived.

This is where Eve got an independent spirit. When God corrected Eve and Adam the discipline was set by God to keep Adam and Eve from having independent spirits.

"...as being heirs together of the grace of life."

Here's a real insight: The church is a primary learning place for the husband and his woman. The home is just as important. Let me explain: Husbands and wives have equal amounts of responsibility and differing accountability although husbands and their wives are both accountable before God. The husband is ultimately responsible to give account to God for the depth and actions of their relationship.

Here's what happens in almost every church on Sunday mornings. The husband and his wife both hear the message the pastor delivered. The wife tells her husband at the end of the service, "I'm going to the bathroom and getting in the car. I'll wait for you." Her husband walks toward the church door and finds a greeting line for the pastor. He waits for his turn in line to shake hands with the pastor. The husband is thinking of something to say. The husband says to the pastor, "Nice sermon! God bless you. Have a good week." That's the end of the conversation. It is so superficial. We need to get past our superficiality and discuss what we learned! The pastor may benefit from it, too, and maybe improve on his message.

Now, the wife exited from another door, got in the family car and started the engine. She fired up the air conditioning. The husband walked toward the car and got in. They started a conversation. "That was a really nice message he gave today," he said. His wife agreed. The husband continued, "He shared a couple of things I felt convicted of. I was short in my temper last week. I didn't feel well at work. I had a lot of stress. I lost control and someone walked away being angry. He didn't talk to me the rest of the week."

"I had the same problem, Dear," the wife said, "It's been so hot this past week. The heat got to me and I actually had the woman in the cubicle next to me start to yell at me. She ticked me off and I responded in kind. We haven't made amends yet."

A connection happened between the couple that couldn't happen in the church meeting. The husband and his woman were connecting with each other in the car. They confessed to each other where they were missing the mark. They let down their guard because they had some intimacy in their relationship. They decided to pray together. Their burdens began to lift.

Communication is one of the hallmarks of a good marriage. Discussion that brings fruitful growth is so important. Yet, couples are out there where the men and their women put church before each other. It doesn't work. Moreover, some people have the wrong motives and strive for attention and leadership in the church more than they strive for having a good marriage. This is not good. Still, other couples get married for the wrong reasons like emotional co-dependence, financial reasons, convenience and more. God can redeem these situations but it takes confession on the part of each spouse and lots of work. Matthew 19:6 says, "Therefore what God has joined together let no man put asunder." I have shared with you some of the importance of communicating between wives and husbands. Husbands and wives can sometimes have their own agenda and improperly feel independent of one another. God put these couples together. Communicate. You'll save yourselves a lot of heartache.

RESTORING COMMUNICATION

Job's fortunes were restored because he was a product of God's love and grace. That's how Job's Point A formed in the first place. He loved God and God blessed him. Yet, it wasn't that simple like the pressing of a button or two and having God's grace pour out. Job amassed many riches because of worship, integrity, hard work and love. He loved other people, even those who were not God's people. None of his three friends were believers but Job took time for them. I heard one prominent Christian leader who instructed his followers to not have close friends who were not Christians. I never liked that. We need to engage people where they are in life. We don't need to withdraw from existing relationships out of fear someone creates because they think it's not healthy. Most of us are mature enough to determine what relationships we can have and their depth. You decide.

Job's pious actions didn't help him at all, like offering for his children's sake or even doing all the right things. Have you ever felt like you have done all the right things and maybe God still didn't bless you? This is because it's not about performance, it's about relationship. Leaders teach new Christians about reading enough, praying enough, witnessing enough in all ways to become better Christians. Although these things are important, we all need these tools to get to know God better. These disciplines are only some of the ways to get to know God better. These tools are only some of the ways to get to know God better. However, God does not grade you using a report card. He accepts you where you are. Your growth comes from meeting God where He is and having Him meet you where you are. There is great growth and maturity in that.

If we are maturing in God, we must be willing to be corrected. Job was willing to do this. Our parents guided us through the process of correction through our childhood. We correct our three-year-old in a much different manner that we correct our 16-year-old. This is because the older children have more capacity to understand the discipline and correction. As I wrote in my book, "Is my Father yet alive?", "No matter how mature we think we are in the Lord we must be open to correction." God helps us get from Point A to Point B by correcting us. He does it as a loving Father, handing out the discipline for us based on what we need to learn. He is not too harsh. Thank God!

BE PREPARED TO DEAL
WITH THE ISSUES

John Maxwell wrote in his book, "Failing Forward" that we were never prepared to deal with failure. Doesn't failure come upon us suddenly sometimes? Maxwell says that coming out of school, he feared it, misunderstood it and ran away from it. He learned to make failure his friend and he can teach you the same.

Have you heard of the Peter Principle? The Peter Principle is a concept by Laurence J. Peter. Employees are promoted based on their success in previous jobs until they reach a level where they are no longer competent (Source: Wikipedia.). This kind of action is found in private industry and in government. This is not a perfect model. A person gets promoted more than once, then suddenly he can't handle the position he was promoted to. Why is that? It's because employees take of paradigms into new positions. It's also because the employees under the managers don't embrace the new paradigms. Almost always an increase in status brings with it an increase in responsibilities. People need to adjust to these responsibilities or possibly lose their jobs. Corporate America and Government are filled with people who don't embrace new paradigms. This holds back productivity and morale. In extreme cases people suffer heart attacks, cancer, strokes and more by internalizing these problems.

These kinds of problems are also faced in marriages. Staleness settles in when one spouse takes the other for granted. Communication wanes. Husbands and wives start paying less attention to each other.

Before you know it one partner starts seeking satisfaction outside the marriage and an affair ensues, all because the old paradigm wasn't working anymore. People always tend to seek a level of satisfactory happiness. It is different for everybody. The new paradigm in a marriage could be for one partner to open a dialog with the other partner or to seek out a pastor or counselor to talk with. If Point A isn't working anymore, it's time to wake up and ask yourself why and also to seek help. So many resources are available and someone you are infatuated with from the opposite sex shouldn't be one of them. Waking up to things not being quite right is actually your alarm going off that your marriage is flat and may dissolve. Don't be afraid. own up to having a problem and face it head on.

WHO CAN WE MARRY?

A lot of controversy surrounds the Christian church today as to what marriage is, why get married and who can we marry. A lot of this controversy is because of societal rebellion against the Establishment. The rebellion began in the 1960's when people started casting off restraint. The teenagers and young adults at that time questioned the value of marriage. A significant number of young people adopted "free love", defined as living together apart from marriage and having open sexual relationships. Sexual activity was at a high rate and marriage was frowned upon.

The Corinthian church had similar questions. A lot of ancient and near ancient societies had the same problems. This is why God addressed His people in the Ten Commandments, saying, "You shall not commit adultery."- Exodus 20:14. An abundance of sexual immorality helps destroy societies.

Paul has a lot to say about marriage and he says it in 1 Corinthians 7. Paul starts out by saying, "It is good for a man not to touch a woman."-1 Corinthians 7:1. " From my experience a lot of men are groaning when they hear this verse, 1 Corinthians 7:1, read aloud in the church. Men think God is taking away men's fun. It's not that way at all. God is looking for character development and the moral preservation of societies. Paul said, "Nevertheless, to avoid fornication, let every man have his own wife, and let every woman have her own husband."-1 Corinthians 7:2.

West Hills Community Church (westhills.org) produced a study on the Internet called, "The Beauty of Marriage". Here is how they explain the situation of sex in the Corinthian church: "Paul corrects a misunderstanding around sex in the Corinthian church where some thought it was holier to abstain even in their marriages. Instead, Paul shows us that sex within marriage helps us avoid temptation, is an opportunity to give and points to a greater intimacy and oneness in new creation."

Paul says that neither the husband nor the wife have authority over their own body.- verse 4. He addresses sexual relations by saying the husband and wife should not deprive each other unless it is by consent for a time so they can give themselves to fasting and prayer.- verse 5. This is a valid point. Sex can easily take over a marriage and be the number one priority in a relationship if we let it. Sex then becomes the arbiter of the values and decisions we make.

The Law Firm Wilkinson and Finkbeiner, LLP cites ten top reasons for divorce. Here are four of them:

- Lack of commitment, 73%, #1
- Infidelity, 55%, #3
- Unrealistic expectations (which I say can be carried into the bedroom), 45%
- Lack of equality in the relationship, (similar to Unrealistic Expectations, in my opinion), 44%

Respondents cited more than one reason for divorce, according to the study. Placing sexual desires under the control of our spirit and our spirit under the control of God's Spirit brings balance. Having self-control in our sex lives prevents sex from being the number one priority and keeps us truly happy.

The apostle speaks by permission. Paul instructs us and leaves room for us to decide and make convictions about what is right. This is the beauty of the scriptures. Sometimes we are left to form our own convictions about matters. This is pointed out so well when the woman caught in adultery was brought to Jesus. Her accusers wanted to convict Jesus of breaking the Law. All of her accusers were convicted when Jesus wrote in the sand, and they all went home from the synagogue. Only Jesus and the woman were left at the synagogue. Jesus said to the woman, "Neither do I condemn you. Go and sin no more."- John 8:11.

The Jews in the synagogue wanted Jesus to condemn the act of adultery and o give the Jewish men the right to stone the woman who was caught. That didn't happen. The scripture says, "For the law made nothing perfect."- Hebrews 7:19. I really don't believe Jesus wrote the Law in the sand in front of His accusers. I do believe that He was writing in the sand and transcending the situation top speak to higher values. Every one of His accusers was convicted in their own spirit. They were convicted in their consciences, a part of their spirits. This is what we need. We need to have convictions about many things, even our salvation. Many people go on an altar call and accept Jesus as their personal Lord and Savior but they never have or develop any convictions to give that decision any holding power. We need convictions about our relationship with our Lord and Savior. We also need convictions about our marriages so they'll be successful and stick.

Concerning divorce, Paul says to not to let the wife depart from her husband. He says this statement came from the Lord. Paul also said if she departed to let her remain unmarried or be reconciled to her. He also said that if the wife is not a believer and she is pleased to dwell with her husband then let her stay in the marriage.

When one of the marriage partners is a believer and the other is not, Paul says that the unbelieving partner is sanctified by the believing partner. Sanctified means two things: 1) They see their love as sept apart by the sacrament of marriage, and 2) They see it as free from being sin or purified. It is not a sin for a believing partner to be married to an unbelieving partner if they were married and one of the partners became a believer. If this was not the case, then the children are sanctified as holy. To be holy means to be set apart. This is very important. Paul wants peace and order in the home.

I do subscribe to the belief that it is not right for a Christian to marry a non-Christian. I will review that shortly.

Paul says we don't know if we can and will lead our unbelieving spouse to the Lord. We have a very limited ability as spouses to do that. Salvation is God's business. We all have experienced telling others about Jesus and having people turn us off. This is deep stuff. We don't lead people to God; God leads them to Himself. He may or may not use us. Moreover, one partner is serving God. The other partner is serving themselves or something else in this case.

Love makes a difference here. Some couples where a non-Christian is married to a Christian have more love than Christian couples. We can't change people. We need to accept them where they are. Some well meaning parents tear apart their children's marriages by constantly correcting them. Paul made this discourse to bring peace to the church at Corinth. We are better examples of Christ's love if we serve to help make marriages succeed.

Paul says in 1 Corinthians 7:25 that he has no commandments from the Lord but he gives his judgment as one who has obtained mercy from the Lord to be faithful. Paul is saying that he has the Lord's permission to speak and that Paul has been faithful to be celibate.

Paul also said the time was short. I want to address this issue from two angles. First of all, Paul may have known Jesus' words from Matthew 24 that the temple would be destroyed with the Jewish and Roman worlds and be thrown into upheaval.

When we put deadlines and urgency in our lives, we increase focus. Paul was trying to put more focus in their marriages by saying the time was short. Many couples today are wondering when all the warring, scamming, reckless driving, bad business practices and the like will ever end. It's more important for couples to focus to focus on their marriages now.

MARRIAGE IS FOR US TO PUT ALL OUR EFFORT INTO NOW

It's not only all of that; marriage isn't forever. Jesus said so in Matthew 24 that we will be like the angels in heaven when we die and we're married. I first heard this message that marriage isn't forever from Apostle Alma Perrin in Lawrenceville, Virginia in 2005. The scripture bore her out. I meditated on this passage and I read the chapter again. I concluded that Apostle Perrin was right. I decided I had to put everything into my marriage right away because it wouldn't last forever. I wound up divorcing, but I put all my effort into making the marriage succeed. My ex-did the best she could to make the marriage work, too. I am remarried now and putting all of my effort into making this new marriage succeed. As for the former marriage I am not going to lay any blame. We both had our part, and we forgave each other for our actions that led to our divorce.

Paul says that anyone who gives his virgin daughter to marriage does well and anyone who does not give his virgin daughter in marriage does better. People get confused here by thinking that giving their daughter in marriage is not good by comparison. That's not what Paul is saying. Paul is approving of marriage. We need to look a little deeper. Yes, a woman does care more for the things of her husband. If her spirit is submitted to God's Spirit and her spirit is ruling over her soul and body along with her husband's spirit submitted to God's Spirit, the marriage is beautiful. Paul is also pointing out that marriage is a challenge. It is difficult to live completely like this all the time. There are distractions.

The apostle concludes by saying the woman and the man "can marry whom they will, only in the Lord."- 1 Corinthians 7:39. Paul spoke by permission and not by commandment. He cited that Christian marriages would save people a lot of trouble with both partners pulling in the same direction toward Christ. That will bring more peace.

We can't automatically pull scripture and automatically say American society is the same way as Corinthian society. We can take some things from the scripture and evaluate what is going on here at home. Examine things carefully.

MARRIAGE IS GOOD AND HONORABLE IN ALL

"Marriage is honorable in all and the bed undefiled."-Hebrews 13:4 The writer of Hebrews completely approves of marriages, even in a situation where a believer is already married to an unbeliever as I mentioned before. How can we get couples going in the right direction in a marriage?

I think this is really important, but we must be careful. This kind of communication can easily become a method of control by the parents. Other people can make the situation to be, "anything goes", and not allow for any accountability at all. A fine line exists. The Hippie movement of the 1960's espoused free love and rebellion against authority. The right line to handle courtship and preparation for marriage has become blurred. It's important, though, to have certain character qualities and provisions for the marriage to work well. I believe this is worthy of discussion between parents and their children with an appropriate atmosphere on the parents' part.

WHAT ABOUT DIVORCE?

I've seen two different Christian camps speak very strongly about divorce. One group says that divorce is entirely not an option for Christian couples. The other group says it's okay to divorce in certain circumstances, like adultery. I heard a woman's message in church sometime ago. She said, "Malachi 2 says God hates divorce, so you shouldn't divorce." I thought about what she said for some time. I came to think that God divorce because divorce caused such pain and grief, not to mention the anguish inflicted upon Israelite society. As I thought about divorce, I knew I would suffer a lot of pain. I knew I would break off a relationship that lasted 30 years including 14 months of courtship. I told people that my divorce was a fate worse than death; that I didn't wish it on my worst enemy. I talked to two Church leaders over time. One said God was angry at me. The other said that I was out of covenant with his church. I learned from both of them that I couldn't please everybody. I learned from my divorce who my friends were and weren't. This was a hard and valuable lesson for me. My relationships with the people who stood by me became even stronger because they accepted me when I was struggling.

People get married for any and every reason. You name it-people get married because one partner did special favors for the other one. Maybe it was for emotional support, sex, money or an arranged marriage like what goes on in other cultures, and more. I remember sitting with my then-wife in my pastor's office one Saturday morning many years ago. We were married one year. We hadn't seen each other much at that time because our work schedules conflicted. We told him our situation. He told us, "You know what your problem is? You've been married for a year! Go home and work things out." I sensed his sarcastic humor. We went home and worked on our relationship.

Lynn Hiles was mentioned earlier in my book. He used to say, "Why not rent an old trailer the first two years of marriage. Then you can kick, scream and throw things at each other without worrying about the value of the trailer." His advice was hilarious. It was also good advice.

Another pastor told my wife and me, "Your marriage is like a box. There is a key that unlocks the box. Tell me what key unlocks the box." He sent my then-wife and me home to pray, fast and find out what key unlocks the box. We came back to his office a week later. He said, "The key which unlocks the box is love." We didn't come up with the right answer. We didn't know where he was headed with his answer. We kept working on our marriage until we separated three years later. It was a terribly hard decision to make. It cost me some of my friendships and some income. It was a most miserable time for me but I came out of it as a stronger man.

"BECAUSE OF YOUR HARDNESS OF HEART..."

In Matthew 19:3 the Pharisees came to Jesus, tempting Him and saying to Him, "Is it lawful for a man to divorce his wife for any reason?"

Jesus answered and said to them, "Have you not read that He who made them at the beginning made them male and female and said, 'For this cause a man shall leave father and mother and shall cling unto his wife, and they two shall be one flesh"? Therefore what God has joined together let not man separate.'

"They said to Him, 'Why did Moses command to give a certificate of divorce and to send her away?'

"He said to them, "Moses, because of the hardness of your hearts.'"- Matthew 19:3-8a.

It was because of the hardness of their hearts that God allowed for divorce. People get married for any and every reason today but they do they get married because God joined them together? Many people pick a spouse like Abraham held up Ishmael before God and said, "O that Ishmael might live before You!"-Genesis 17:18. It doesn't work because it's not God's way. 1 Corinthians 7:27 says, "Are you bound to a wife? Do not seek to be released." We can interpret that verse to say God will bring you a spouse.

COMPLETING MY STORY

I mentioned when I began my story that I was divorced and remarried. I did feel qualified to write a book on marriage. I learned that marriage was a good thing! I was interested in marrying again if I found the right person. My divorce became final in May 2012. I started dating again in December that year. The first dating relationship didn't last long. I was overemotional.

I ventured into dating online. I met one girl in early Spring one year. She was a professional woman from Northern Virginia. I thought it would be fun to go out with her. She suggested that we eat Easter Dinner at a Marriott Hotel near where she lived. The meal was supposed to cost $40. The bill came. It totaled $170.23! She acted like she was aghast. "Oh, I'm sorry," she said. "Let's split the bill in half." I agreed. It was the last time I would go out with her. My ride back to Baltimore and my house was a long one. I learned a lesson about communication and responsibility.

Then there was this one girl who was so much fun. I found another girl online and I started chatting with her one evening. Within two nights she asked me to chat with her every night before she went to bed. She went to bed really early because she was a nurse and had to get up, exercise and start work early in the mornings. We had lots of fun chatting. We had each other's phone number and we started watching NCIS from our home locations on Tuesday nights. She always solved the crime long before I did. She was quite smart and had a well-developed intuition.

We chatted on a Friday night two weeks before Thanksgiving. We had already been talking for eight weeks. She asked, "When are you going to ask me out?"

I told her, "I was going to ask you out tonight!" I figured I had to ask her out that night or I wasn't going to have a relationship with her. I put a plan together to pick her up At her home, take her to a Swiss Village of shops, eat lunch at a wonderful restaurant and eat dinner together.

I met her mid-Saturday morning the Saturday before Thanksgiving. It was unusually mild that day. I met her in Southern Pennsylvania. It was 65 degrees. The Swiss Village was full of shops with upstairs apartments above each ship. All the shops were quite interesting. I said on the way to the restaurant that I wanted to eat at the luncheonette instead. I told her I was having a really good time and that my stomach would be too full to enjoy myself the rest of the day if I ate at the restaurant. We each ate some broasted chicken, some corn and some mashed potatoes. The luncheonette was owned by the restaurant. The food was really good.

We got in the car after we ate lunch. She asked me if we could drive some 15 miles or so to her jewelry store. She wanted some rings sized. I walked around the mall where the jewelry store for one-half hour. She caught up with me outside, spun me around and said, "Isn't this the best date you ever had?"

I was beside myself. No girl ever talked to me like that before. I felt lie saying to her in Pumbaa's voice in the movie, "The Lion King", "Are you talking to me?"

"Well, yeah," I told her. I took my time replying because I was savoring what she said.

"How do you think it was so," she asked. This girl was quite intelligent and thoughtful. She knew how to play up the emotions of the moment.

"I said, "It's 65 degrees and it's the Saturday before Thanksgiving. A lot of people are out on their first date. They're asking each other, 'What's your favorite color,' 'What's your favorite car,' and so on.

We've been taking with each other for two months and we have been very comfortable with each other. We've having a good time."

"I guess you're right," she said with a big smile. We hugged as we walked toward the car, got in and headed out to dinner. Dinner was quite relaxing.

We dated for ten months. We were boyfriend and girlfriend. I knew we weren't going to be married. We agreed to not get married but I really enjoyed her company. We went to the movies. We ate lunch and dinner out often. Sometimes we just talked.

The takeaway for me was that this relationship was a great experience. I also learned some depth about what a good relationship was like. That's important, too. Some people date the person they're going to marry. That works sometimes but it doesn't work all the time. 1 Corinthians 7:39 says that a woman can marry whom she will; only in the Lord. Again, Paul said it by permission.

I've had good experiences and bad experiences in dating and trying to find the right one. This is sometimes painful but this is the way we find the one person God gave to us to marry. This how we find our values, beliefs, dislikes and our values. Breakups can be hard. I have experienced some of them. Let me say that is far better to experience a breakup before marriage than afterward. I have said a couple of times after a breakup, "Glad I know now." I don't say it out of bitterness. I say it from reaching a good decision.

LEAVING WITH A COMMENT

Christian marriage is wonderful if it is done the right way. Matthew 19:5b says, "The two shall become one flesh, and he who is joined to the Lord is one spirit." I'm talking in practice. Our spirit joined to the Lord is one spirit. Our spirit is submissive to His Spirit. I mentioned that our spirit is made up of three parts: worship, conscience and intuition. Our worship salutes God. Our conscience tells us it's the right thing to do and our intuition tells us Jesus is the right Spirit. When we realize this in our marital relationships, we really have something and we eat from Jesus, the Tree of Life. "For our fellowship (communion, common union) is with the Father and His Son Jesus Christ. If we walk in the light (that He is in the Father and the Son) as He is in the Light, we have fellowship (communion, common union) with one another. And the blood of Jesus cleanses us from every sin (missing the mark so as not to share in the high calling of God in Jesus Christ in knowing Him intimately). – 1 John 1:7

Have at it. Place this into your marriages. Amen.

ATTRIBUTION

John Maxwell, Author, Speaker- pages 16, 48

Lynn Hiles, Leader, Lynn Hiles ministries,- pages 16, 48, 62

David Robinson, Pastor, Community Christian Church- page 16

Zig Ziglar, Author, Speaker, page 22

Albert Meyers, Pastor (deceased), page 27

VinesoftheYaraValley.au, Website, p.32

Laurence Peter, The Peter Principle, page 48

Law Firm of Wilkinson and Finkbeiner, LLP, website, page

Apostle Alma Perrin, page 57

ABOUT RICHARD SZALECKI

Richard Szalecki became a Christian in 1976 when he learned that his religious good deeds couldn't save him. He learned that the religious good works he grew up with believing that they would save him fell short. He found out that salvation was a free gift to those who believed. Richard accepted Jesus Christ as his personal Lord and Savior.

God started teaching Richard through the Bible right away. He picked up important truths and implemented them in his life. He learned that the Spirit of God searches the deep things of God and reveals them to us by His Spirit, comparing spiritual words with spiritual truths.

Szalecki has deep care for people, having served as a Deacon, Lead Deacon, on a Church Council, as an elder in an Elder-Led Church and as an Evangelist. A former pastor has said to his congregation that he has met no one who cared more for people than Rick Szalecki.

"Think Outside the Box Concerning Marriage" is Richard Szalecki's third book. His other two books are "Think Outside the Box" (currently out of print) and "Is my Father yet alive?" a Bible Study book about Joseph of the Old Testament.

Szalecki has two grown children. He lives with his current wife Cheryl near Fort Walton Beach, Florida.

Printed in the United States
by Baker & Taylor Publisher Services